Illustrated
Canal Fishing Diaries

Thank you for purchasing this book.

You can find **more fishing books by this author** by scanning the QR code below with your phone's camera (which will take you to the **Author's Amazon page**).

Mark's website: www.000Fishing.com

Mark's YouTube channel: https://www.youtube.com/@000fishing

CONTENTS

WHERE IT ALL STARTED

I was brought up in Blackburn, in northwest England, where the Leeds and Liverpool Canal flowed through the town and was a short walk from where I lived.

As the name implies, the canal connects the cities of Leeds in the east and Liverpool in the west. Construction began in 1770 and took nearly 50 years to complete. The completed canal is 127 miles long and contains over 90 locks.

I started fishing the canal when I was in my teens, over 45 years ago. The canal in Blackburn was typical of an urban canal, with plenty of floating tyres and rusted prams.

Fishing the canal near my home in the 1970's

A series of locks near the old Blackburn Royal Infirmary were a five-minute walk from home, and I spent many happy hours catching stone loach in the fast-flowing sections of the lock run-offs, as well as gudgeon and the occasional roach in the sections beneath the locks.

As I grew older, I used to take the bus out of town and escape into the countryside. Here, the canal appeared cleaner, with reeds and lilies, and was a much more relaxing place to fish.

Some of my fondest memories are of fishing here with my grandad, aka 'Gramps'. I used to drag him hundreds of metres down the canal to find the best fishing spots. We enjoyed catching a few fish, including roach, gudgeon, and perch.

In my late teens, I began match fishing on the canal. My local fishing club held regular matches on Wednesday evenings and Saturdays. Matches were popular, attracting up to thirty anglers.

The match fishing scene also led me to another Northwest canal, the Lancaster Canal, which connects Preston with an area north of Lancaster. The 'Lanky', as it is known, is a shallower canal that runs through picturesque countryside. To me, it was a magical canal, very different from the deeper, more urban canal where I began fishing.

The Lanky contained skimmer bream, a species that, at the time, I rarely saw in local stretches of the Leeds and Liverpool Canal.

The Lanky was a popular spot for match fishing, with large matches drawing hundreds of anglers. The standards were very high. When I was fishing a match on the Lanky, angling legends Kevin Ashurst and Ian Heaps (England Internationals and World Champions) walked past me while heading to their pegs a little further down the canal. I was 'star-struck', but I managed to say a nervous 'hello' to each of them.

Dave Roper, another angler who went on to win the World Championship, was a regular on the bank. I got to know him a little and sat behind him to watch him fish matches on a few occasions.

Me with the lads from the two local match fishing teams

Over the next few years, match fishing became my first love. I won several junior matches on the canal, including the Blackburn Junior Canal Championship, the club's junior leagues, and a few senior matches. I also captained the Northern Anglers Junior Match Squad at the Junior National Championship in Lincolnshire on the Sibsey Trader and Hobhole Drains, where I won my section. It was an extremely proud moment.

After I started working, earning money, and discovering girls and beer, I began to do less match fishing. I went fishing, but not as intensely as in previous years.

Over the next few decades, fishing would remain an important part of my life, but I no longer fished matches. I expanded my fishing knowledge by exploring various venues and techniques. I stopped canal fishing to explore rivers and lakes, and I even started fly fishing, which I've grown to enjoy.

In January 2023, I turned sixty years old. For my birthday, I decided to fish a match on my local canal, 40 years after my last canal fishing match.

The weather was cold and windy. The canal had thawed after being frozen for several weeks. In the next chapter, I explain what happened.

That day, I renewed my interest in canal fishing. Since then, I've explored the Leeds, Liverpool, and Lancaster Canals. I've been astounded by the size and variety of fish that inhabit my local waters.

I have documented some of these trips on my YouTube channel, 000Fishing, and I decided to write this little book about my canal fishing adventures, which I hope will inspire you to try canal fishing if you haven't already.

FORTY YEARS ON

Location: Leeds and Liverpool Canal, near Blackburn.

Date: 29th January 2023

Air Temp: 6°C

Fishing match.

For my 60th birthday, I decided to revisit my youth and fish a match. Forty years after my last match on the canal.

Background

I chose to celebrate my 60th birthday by entering a local canal fishing match. The location was an area where I had fished on several occasions, but I hadn't fished there for many years.

The match length was pegged along an area used to moor boats, and there was a wide area (or basin) that was part of the boatyard, which was to be included in the match. Boatyards are good fish-holding areas in winter, and basins can hold large shoals of better-quality fish, such as bream.

A week or so before the match, I decided to go for a practice session. However, when I got to the canal, the canal was completely frozen over. I revisited it several days later with the same result. So, practicing was not possible.

I talked to an old match-fishing buddy of mine, 'Ditch', and he gave me a few pointers.

Catches of Bream had won several of the previous matches at the venue. There were also small roach and perch to target.

Match Day

I turned up early and parked in the carpark, opposite the match length. I have to admit to feeling a little nervous. Not having fished a match for so long.

I might have felt more confident if I had had the opportunity to practice before hand. Never mind.

I had tied up a few pole rigs and other gear and got a selection of bait.

The Draw and Peg

The match organiser and other competitors started to arrive and made me feel welcome. We paid our match fees, and then the draw was made.

I was pegged a short walk from the car park on a fairly narrow section, with boats opposite. The favourite pegs were the ones in the basin area, but I was a good distance away from them. Oh well, I'll make the best of it and enjoy my birthday on the bank.

Conditions

The weather was blustery, and the air temperature was low. The canal was cold and very clear. I could see patches of underwater weed, and the far side of the peg near the boats looked shallow, and I could see the bottom. The nearside was the same; I could see the bottom several metres out from the bank.

Tactics

I decided to target three areas of the peg: 1—near the boats opposite, where I would feed casters; 2—down the deepest part of the canal, feeding chopped worm; and 3—a few metres in front of me, feeding liquidised bread.

Gear

Pole with three top kits set up for each of the target areas.

Bait

Breadpunch, worms, casters, and some corn.

The Match

I kicked things off by feeding a few casters across the canal and potting in some chopped worms down the deepest part of the canal. I then fed a small ball of liquidised bread a few metres in front of me and made my first drop in over the liquidised bread, with a small piece of punched bread on the hook.

I anticipated an instant bite, which is normally the case when breadpunch fishing. Nothing! Ten minutes went by without a bite. The wheels were already coming off the little match plan I had in my head.

I continued to fire a few casters across and then decided to drop onto the chopped worm line, with a Dendrobaena worm on the hook. First bite: a little perch. Then another, a bit bigger, which I netted.

Perch came sporadically throughout the match. When this line went quiet, I tried caster on the hook, fishing across to the boats. No bites at all on casters.

I again tried breadpunch, without a bite – strange.

Looking up and down the match length, no one seemed to be catching much. I continued to catch little perch on worms, and then I hooked into something heavy. I saw a big bream turn under the water, and then disaster. It snapped my line! I'm not sure exactly why this happened. I was fishing a fine hook length, but it should have been strong enough to handle a bream. Maybe the line had been damaged beforehand.

The peg went quiet, and there were no more signs of bream. I dropped back onto my breadpunch line for the last thirty minutes of the match and surprisingly caught several small roach, which had been absent earlier in the day.

Word along the bank was that it had been a tough day for everyone.

Eventually, the scales reached me, and I weighed in 1lb 10oz of small perch and roach. Enough to win the match.

I'd won a canal fishing match on my 60th birthday, forty years after fishing my last canal fishing match.

I was overjoyed.

60th Birthday - Match winning net 1lb 10oz

SURPRISES

Location: Leeds and Liverpool Canal, near Padiham.

Date: 28th May 2023

Air Temp: 16°C

Following the fishing match, and despite having my interest in canal fishing rekindled, I spent the next few months mostly river fishing.

I like to vary my fishing and the species that I target based on the seasons. Fishing for chub and grayling in winter, and then stick float fishing for dace and roach up until the end of the river fishing season. Then, at the end of the coarse river fishing season, I fly fish for brown trout for a while.

So, it was May before I got back onto the canal.

Background

I'd spotted a section of canal that looked interesting while travelling along a local road and made a mental note to explore it one day.

Gear

I found a place to park, not far from the canal, and took my lightweight fishing gear, a rucksack, and a chair, rather than the heavy seat box I'd used on my canal fishing match. I had a short waggler rod and a light feeder rod in my bag.

Conditions

The weather was cool but pleasant. It was a bright day, with clouds in the sky. The place that I decided to fish had yellow iris growing along the towpath. The canal was quite clear and weedy in parts, and there were islands of floating weed that moved up and down with the flow of the canal.

Bait

Sweetcorn. Sensas - Gros Gardons groundbait.

Tactics

I decided to start off float fishing, using a small waggler and a single piece of corn on a size 14 hook. I fed a few grains of sweetcorn, and because of the clarity of the water, I chose to fish down the middle of the canal in the deepest water.

I continued to feed a few pieces of sweetcorn every ten minutes, or so.

The Fishing

It took an hour to get my first bite and I was hooked into a heavy nodding 'lump', a bream, around 3 and a half pounds, which came to the net. Excellent.

I quickly returned it and carried on fishing. There were no more bites for about an hour, and then my float disappeared, and I was hooked into something different. It took off down the canal and then went into some weeds, and then the hook pulled out. What was that?

Thirty more minutes went by, and I hooked another one. After a short battle, a tench of around three and a half pounds slid into my landing net. My first-ever tench from the Leeds and Liverpool Canal.

After that, the swim went quiet for around an hour and a half. The floating weed had now made float fishing almost impossible, so I decided to dig out my feeder rod.

I realised that the only feeder in my bag was a tiny hybrid feeder, and I didn't have any short hooklinks or any pellets with me.

So, I tied a standard size 14 hook onto a four-inch hooklink, mixed up a bit of Gros Gardons ground bait, and stuck a piece of sweetcorn directly onto the hook. I filled the feeder with the sweetcorn hidden inside the dome of groundbait and did a short underarm cast.

Next time, I'd be better prepared, but for now, this would have to do.

Twenty minutes later, the quivertip hooped around, and I was attached to another bream, this time slightly smaller than the first one.

I had made that my last cast and packed up with a smile on my face.

Three nice fish from a new stretch of canal, including my biggest ever bream and my first-ever tench from the canal.

I realised that fishing on my local canal had changed enormously since my teenage years. No longer were small roach and gudgeon the target, but now there were some clonking bream and tench present. What a nice surprise!

EVENING SESSION WITH GARY & MITSY

Location: Leeds and Liverpool Canal, near Padiham.

Date: 2nd June 2023

Air Temp: 20°C

Background

Earlier in the week, I'd been talking to a friend of mine, Gary, about the great fishing on the canal. Keen to explore the stretch, we arranged to meet up on Friday afternoon and fish into the early evening.

Gary has a YouTube channel (details at the end of this chapter), and I had recently started my own YouTube channel. On this day, we wouldn't be filming. Instead, it was to be a little social fishing session.

Until I started creating YouTube fishing videos, I didn't realise how much effort goes into making films. Preparing cameras, setting them up, and making sure the sound is okay. It all takes time and can be very disruptive to your fishing. It is enjoyable, but filming your fishing trips for YouTube is different from just fishing.

On this session, we could focus purely on fishing and chatting.

Conditions

It was a lovely sunny evening, and we walked further up from where I'd fished on my last session in order to avoid the large patches of floating weed. The water had a tinge of colour, and we could see a few bream basking near the surface.

Gear

I set up my short waggler rod. In fact, it was still set up from the previous trip. Gary had a similar set-up and a feeder rod set-up.

Bait

Dendrobaena worms and sweetcorn. Gary had casters and maggots.

Tactics

I decided to lose feed sweetcorn in the deepest part of the canal, which in my case was just this side of the middle of the canal.

I also thought I'd try feeding chopped worm and fishing worm on the hook, fishing about a rod and a half out from the bank.

Having had experience hooking tench on past sessions, I was fishing quite heavily and using a 3 lb hooklink and a size 12 hook.

Gary opted to fish more finely, with smaller hooks and finer hooklinks.

The Fishing

I started out by fishing sweetcorn on the hook, a bait that had been successful on this stretch before. A couple of hours went by without a bite. I had hoped that the bream and tench would find it irresistible. Not today. Time for a change.

Desperate for a bite, I thought I'd stick a worm on the hook and go for perch. Earlier, I'd fed chopped worm into the swim in front of me. When targeting perch with a worm, I like to fish a worm several inches off the bottom. This way, I think that the worm hangs tantalisingly and attracts the attention of perch.

I cast out, with the hook bait hanging about a foot from the bottom of the canal. Instant bite, a small perch, and then a run of perch, quickly taking the tally to a dozen fish up to ten ounces. Interestingly, one of the perch coughed up a dead roach, which it had previously eaten.

I was finally catching some fish, but then the swim went quiet.

I fished on for a few minutes and then decided to feed some more chopped worm. Minutes after this, the float buried itself under the surface, and I hooked into a powerful fish. I wondered if it could be a big perch.

After taking me up and down the swim for a while, the fish surfaced—a chunky tench. Excellent.

Meanwhile, Gary, on the next peg, had managed to catch a couple of skimmers. They were obviously in the area but had avoided my sweetcorn bait, thicker hooklinks, and larger hooks. Gary's more delicate approach and maggot hookbaits looked like they were the way to catch the skimmers today. When bites dried up on his skimmer line, Gary cast across to the other side of the canal and started to catch perch one after the other.

Fishing with others allows you to accelerate your understanding of how to fish different waters, especially when you fish using different baits and tactics. You learn from each other.

Shortly after returning my tench, I recast and soon hooked into another fish that gave me the run-around. Another tench. A bigger, stockier fish, which looked like a football, with big shoulders and a big, humped back. Terrific.

With the sun now dipping towards the horizon, we decided to pack up.

I took a picture of the sunset and headed back to the car.

It had been another fascinating day on the canal.

YouTube

You can find Gary's YouTube channel here:

https://www.youtube.com/@garywilliamsandmitsy

PERCH TRICKERY

Location: Leeds and Liverpool Canal, near Accrington

Date: 11th June 2023

Air Temp: 22°C

Background

I decided to explore a new section of the canal near Accrington, a couple of miles away from where I had been fishing on my previous sessions.

The section was quite sheltered and had tree cover on the far bank and hedges at the back of the towpath.

I wanted to see if I could catch bream or a tench from this new area.

Conditions

The day was mild, with blue skies and an intermittent breeze.

I noticed that the canal in this area was much more coloured than it had been on my canal fishing trips, possibly due to the higher levels of weekend boat traffic.

Gear

The rod I set up was an 11-foot float rod with a small crystal waggler, 3-pound line, and a size 10 hook.

Bait

Sweetcorn and a few worms.

Tactics

I wanted to target bream and tench, so rather than fishing maggots, which would likely attract roach, I fed a small handful of sweetcorn across the canal, near the overhanging trees. I also put a smaller amount, about a rod and a half out, to the right of where I was sitting.

I continued to loose feed corn on both lines throughout the day.

The Fishing

Despite conditions looking good, and although continuing to try both the far side line and the nearside one, and regularly putting a few grains of sweetcorn into each swim, I was biteless for two and a half hours.

During the day, several boats passed by and clouded up the peg. It seemed that the canal bottom here was very silty, and plumes of light-coloured (almost sandy-coloured) silt hung in the water long after the boats had passed by.

Sometimes, this can encourage shy fish to feed, but not today.

I was staring a 'blank' in the face.

In my bag, I noticed I had a small tub that contained a handful of worms, which had been left over from a previous trip.

I hadn't got enough worms to try a favourite canal fishing tactic—feeding chopped worms. I only had enough for hookbait.

So, I decided to employ an 'old-school trick'.

In the late 1970's, we often fed garden peat when fishing for skimmers and perch. It attracts fish without feeding them.

The worms were stored in soil, and so I decided to use this soil as a groundbait. I put a couple of handfuls of soil into a bait box and added water to create a slop.

Not only would the slop create visible attraction in the form of a black cloud, but the soil would contain worm flavours as worms had been living in it for some time.

I threw in a couple of small balls of the slop and cast out a worm, which fell through the black cloud.

The float immediately slipped away, and a small perch was on the end of my line.

Each time I cast in; a perch grabbed the worm. It was a perch every cast for the next thirty or forty minutes.

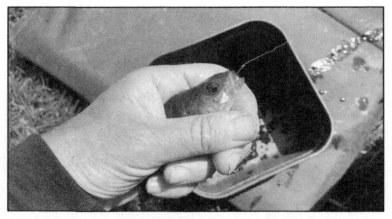

This 'old-school trick' worked well and helped me avoid a blank.

I WASN'T EXPECTING THAT!

Location: Leeds and Liverpool Canal, near Blackburn

Date: 16th July 2023

Air Temp: 14°C

Background

I ventured back onto the canal in an area that I'd not fished before. The peg I chose was not far from a wide (basin), which was currently not fishable as it was entirely covered in weed.

I thought that the basin might be a good holding spot for shoals of bream, so I set up near to it, hoping to attract them using breadflake on the hook and feeding liquidised bread. Tench were also present in the area, so there was a chance of a bonus tench, too.

I decided to hedge my bets by also taking worms, which I'd use as chopped worm feed and hookbait.

Conditions

It was a cool, overcast day. Rainy and breezy, with occasional strong gusts of wind. The canal was very clear. Some patches of floating weed were present.

Gear

My usual set-up of a waggler rod, a crystal waggler float, 3 lb mainline and hooklink, and a size 12 hook.

Bait

Feed: Liquidised bread and chopped worm. Hook baits: Breadflake and worms.

Tactics

My plan was to fish two lines: a swim two-thirds of the way across the canal, where I would feed a couple of balls of liquidised bread and use breadflake on the hook.

By using breadflake on the hook, I hoped to attract a bream or tench.

I'd leave this swim alone for an hour, hoping that fish would find the liquidised bread and settle over it to feed confidently.

The other swim was close-in, where I'd feed chopped worms and fish with a worm on the hook. In this swim, I would target perch, or tench if they were present.

I'd fish the nearside swim for an hour before trying the furthest one, where I'd fed the liquidised bread.

The Fishing

Although I expected a fairly instant response to my worm, nothing happened.

During the morning, as the light levels increased, I could see that the canal was very clear, just like tap water.

Disappointingly, I could see no fish present in my nearside swim where I'd fed the chopped worm.

The water clarity meant that potentially, the fish could see me on the bank and therefore might be further out, in the deeper water, where there was more cover and where they'd feel safer.

So, I fed some more chopped worm, this time a bit further out, in slightly deeper water. I adjusted my depth and cast out over the newly fed area.

The float disappeared and a perch had grabbed the bait.

Another small perch followed and then I hooked something bigger.

A perch of around a pound gave me a good scrap, but just as it was about to reach the net, it came off. Bugger!

As usual, I was using barbless hooks, and this does occasionally happen.

After an hour had elapsed, I swapped to breadflake on the hook and cast over the area where I'd fed the liquidised bread.

I could see a bright glow on the bottom of the canal where I'd fed my liquidised bread. I wondered if this might actually spook the fish rather than attract them.

I couldn't see any bream milling around the swim. I carried on fishing the swim for another twenty minutes before giving up on it and returning to my nearside swim with a worm on the hook. A few more perch followed.

Then, a bit of drama. A gust of wind scooped up my fishing brolly and hurled it into the canal and it started floating on the surface like a sailboat.

I'd been lazy and not properly pegged it down, and now I was paying the price. What a numpty!

It floated across to the other side of the canal and was unreachable.

Fortunately, the brolly eventually drifted to the towpath side of the canal, and a kind chap retrieved it for me.

I filmed the whole spectacle and later put it on my YouTube channel (it received 43K views, and now the world knows I'm a numpty).

I took a picture of the final net of my little perch and vowed that from now on I'd make sure my brolly was securely pinned down!

TRYING SOMETHING NEW

Location: Leeds and Liverpool Canal, near Blackburn

Date: 27th July 2023

Air Temp: 18°C

Background

I started fly-fishing about three years ago. It was a way of staying in touch with the rivers where I often fished (the Ribble and the Calder), targeting the colourful, hard-fighting trout that live there, and at the same time learning something new.

I taught myself to cast a fly by watching YouTube videos and got into all sorts of tangles during the first year! I should have taken lessons; I would have made much faster progress.

Early on, I rarely caught fish, but I enjoyed trying and the fact that I could travel very light with very little gear.

I slowly improved and now regularly catch fish. My casting still isn't great, but I get by, and I've grown to adore fly-fishing, and eagerly look forward to the start of the brown trout season each year.

Always enjoying a fishing challenge, I set myself the task of trying to catch roach on the canal fly-fishing, something that I'd not tried before.

Would I succeed?

Conditions

A mild day. Cloudy with some patches of blue sky. Occasionally breezy.

The water was crystal clear, with lots of sub-surface weed and patches of floating weed.

Gear

I ventured onto a stretch of my local canal with my lightweight fly-fishing gear (3 weight 7ft Shakespeare Sigma rod).

I'd spotted shoals of roach basking on the surface during a recent recce of the stretch. I wondered if they'd take dry flies.

Tactics

I had a few tiny flies in my box, sparkle gnats, black gnats, and some black midge patterns tied to size 20 hooks.

My plan was to walk up the canal and cast to any roach that I could see topping.

The first fly that I tried was a small sparkle gnat, one of my favourite dry flies.

The Fishing

The majority of my early casts were ignored. Once or twice, a roach would swim up to the fly and then turn away.

If I cast too many times in the direction of a shoal, they'd spook and disappear, so I kept walking along the stretch looking for fish.

Polarising glasses are a must for spotting fish as well as protecting your eyes from wayward dry flies. With the water being so clear, the fish were easy to spot, but I'd only see a handful of fish rise. I'd not seen any fly activity either.

Most of the roach seemed to be hanging around under the patches of floating weed, which made casting to them impossible.

I walked further along the towpath and spotted a shoal out in the open.

I decided to change my fly and put on a black gnat.

My first cast with the new fly resulted in a small roach 'nosing' it but not fully committing to taking it. At least this looked more promising.

Next cast, and one of the slightly bigger fish in the shoal of roach that I cast towards took the fly, and it was on!

I'm not sure whether it was the switch to the new fly or whether the fish had just switched on to feeding on flies, but I continued to catch more small roach for the next hour or so.

It was fun to see the roach take the fly in the clear water of the canal.

I continued walking the canal towpath and casting to groups of fish.

Not only was the fly fishing enjoyable but it was also a good way of exploring the stretch, spotting fish, and discovering underwater features thanks to my polarising glasses.

I always enjoy new fishing challenges, and although I struggled at the start, I managed to catch a few little roach on a new technique.

I know that I have a lot to learn about fly-fishing on canals. But I learned a lot today and will try it again when the conditions are right.

I also have in mind a challenge to catch perch and pike using streamer-pattern flies. I'll try that sometime in the future.

BIG CANAL ROACH

Location: Leeds and Liverpool Canal, near Blackburn

Date: 30th July 2023

Air Temp: 18°C

Background

Today's plan was to try and catch bream and perch. I had previously fished the stretch with a fly rod and caught roach. Today, I'd hunt for other species.

Conditions

The day was cloudy with a few patches of blue sky. An occasional breeze rippled the canal's surface. At the start of the session, the canal was extremely clear.

Gear

Waggler rod, crystal waggler float, 3lb mainline, 2 ½lb hooklink, size 14/12 hooks.

Bait

Sweetcorn and worm hook baits. A dark, natural groundbait. A few 2 mm pellets as feed.

Tactics

I fed two lines: one with chopped worm on the nearside, where I will use a worm as hook bait. I fed another line two-thirds of the way across the canal with a couple of balls of groundbait, containing a few pellets and sweetcorn. Here, I will use sweetcorn as hook bait.

After feeding the groundbait, I will leave this line alone and unfished for an hour while starting on my nearside line.

The Fishing

My first cast was over the chopped worm, but my float didn't settle properly. A perch had grabbed the worm as it fell through the water.

My next fish was a roach on the worm, which leapt acrobatically out of the water when I hooked it.

Following this, several perch appeared in quick succession. Perch are voracious and aggressive feeders who provide excellent sport.

After an hour, I decided to switch to sweetcorn hook bait and have a cast over the line where I'd fed the groundbait.

Fifteen minutes went by without a bite, so I swapped back to a worm on the hook and tried my nearside swim again, and I had several more perch.

Two boats went through the swim. The first moved slowly, while the second, a large barge, moved faster and churned up the bottom, leaving huge brown clouds of silt in the water.

Once the canal had stopped moving and churning, I fed another ball of groundbait into the swim two-thirds across the canal.

I cast over the baited swim with sweetcorn on the hook and missed an 'unmissable' bite.

Shortly afterwards, I hooked what I thought was a skimmer, but it turned out to be a big roach. Excellent.

It was a fin-perfect fish weighing 12–14 oz, and aside from a roach I caught in the 1970s, it was the largest roach I'd ever caught from this canal.

Over the next couple of hours, I had a succession of similar-sized fish.

I also had a lot of missed bites, which I believe were caused by smaller roach grabbing the hookbait but not fully taking it into their mouths.

I ended the day with a net of beautiful roach and small perch.

The size of the roach were an unexpected bonus. The sweetcorn helped avoid the smaller roach that would probably have been first on the bait if I was fishing with maggots.

It's a bait I'll be using again to target big canal roach in the future.

BREAM BONANZA CUT SHORT

Location: Leeds and Liverpool Canal, near Padiham

Date: 11th August 2023

Air Temp: 21°C

Background

I planned to revisit a stretch of canal where I'd in the past caught bream and tench. Today, when I arrived at the stretch, I noticed that the floating weed had worsened. It was now entirely covering the surface of the canal where I'd previously fished.

This time, I chose to walk the opposite direction, down the towpath and found a stretch free from weed.

Conditions

A mild but overcast day with a gentle breeze.

Gear

Waggler rod, 3lb mainline, 3lb pound hooklink, size 12 hook.

Bait

Feed: dark, natural groundbait, laced with sweetcorn. Worms and sweetcorn for hookbaits.

Tactics

I set up on the outside of a slight bend on the canal. When I plumbed up, I found that the water was a bit deeper than the areas I'd fished in the past.

I mixed up some dark, natural groundbait and added corn to the mix. I fed three tangerine-sized balls of bait down the middle in the deepest area of the canal.

I set my waggler float a few inches over depth.

The Fishing

I put a piece of sweetcorn on the hook and eagerly cast it out. The float settled, and nothing happened.

After 30 minutes, I switched to worm on the hook and recast. Another ten minutes passed, and then the float sank.

I struck and hit solid resistance. I could see the golden flank of a good-sized bream twist and turn underwater.

I slipped my landing net under it and put it onto my awaiting unhooking mat. What a cracker!

I put the bream into my keepnet and recast with a worm. Another 15 minutes went by, and then the float sailed away. This time, I landed a nice skimmer.

The swim then went quiet, and shortly after this, a boat went through the swim. It glided past, hardly disturbing the water.

Another ten minutes passed, and I decided to feed another tangerine-sized ball of my groundbait mix.

I glanced down at my keepnet, and visible in the clear water was a large pike staring at the two fish I had inside. It continued peering at the fish through the mesh, and then it eventually disappeared.

Fifteen minutes later, and I was into another skimmer. A similar size to the previous one.

Although I occasionally tried a piece of corn on the hook, the bream wanted worms.

Next cast, a big bream, of around four pounds.

Every twenty minutes or so, I'd get a bite. A couple more skimmers came to the net. All of them were decent fish of around one and a half pounds.

I also had a couple of small roach. I was astounded that they could fit the worm hook bait in their mouths.

Unfortunately, the dreaded floating weed, which had been threatening to invade my swim for the last hour, now engulfed my baited area.

Fishing was no longer possible.

I pulled out my keepnet and was very happy with the result. Two good bream, five skimmers, and a couple of roach.

MICRO LURE FISHING

Location: Leeds and Liverpool Canal, near Accrington

Date: 27th August 2023

Air Temp: 16°C

Background

I got into lure fishing with soft plastic baits several years ago, enjoying both drop-shotting and fishing with small, soft plastic shads on jig heads.

This type of fishing doesn't require you to carry lots of gear, enabling you to travel light and explore lots of water.

A short rod, a small tackle bag, a compact unhooking mat, and a telescopic landing net are all that you need. It is easy to carry and can be stored in your car's boot for spontaneous fishing sessions.

As I only had a couple of hours of free time, I opted to explore a stretch of canal not far from my home.

Conditions

The canal was very clear and weedy. I could see shoals of small roach and the occasional small perch.

The weather was cool with the occasional light breeze.

Later on, the rain started, and the wind increased.

Gear

Sakura rod, Fox Prism reel, Braided line/fluorocarbon leader, Fox Rage lure bag and unhooking mat, telescopic landing net, with rubber mesh head. Polarising glasses.

Bait

Box of tiny soft-plastic lures, including tiny fish patterns and grub style lures.

Tactics

My plan was to walk the stretch, looking for fish activity and likely fish-holding areas.

Wearing my polarising glasses, I could see through the surface glare of the water and see underwater features, as well as any nearby fish.

I'd use a tiny jig head and try the different soft-plastic lures I had with me.

The Fishing

I could see lots of very small roach in the clear water. It was amusing to see them follow the tiny, fish-shaped lure as I moved it through the water.

Where you find shoals of small roach, the perch are usually not far away.

It wasn't long before the lure was grabbed by a greedy perch, which dropped off before I could land it.

I caught another small perch on my next cast, which dropped off onto the grass at my feet.

Sometimes, the small perch grab the end of the lure and aren't hooked properly.

I returned the perch to the water, moved further up the bank, and recast.

I investigated likely-looking spots as I walked along the towpath, exploring the stretch of canal.

Several more perch took the fish-shaped lure. It was good fun.

I wondered if I could tempt a roach by changing to one of the grub-style lures and even bit a piece off it to make it look more like a maggot.

I cast into several shoals of roach, hoping to entice one. Several roach investigated the tiny lure but never took it.

I eventually gave up on the idea and switched back to a full-sized grub lure.

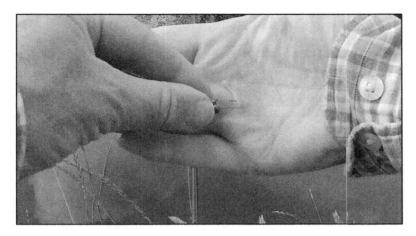

I alternated between the pink and white-coloured grub lures, taking perch on both colours.

It seemed like whatever I cast out would attract the attention of a perch.

I kept walking and casting.

I spotted a couple of bigger perch close to the bank and cast out one of my white grubs. I watched the bigger perch turn and grab the lure, and it was on!

By far, this was the biggest perch of the day.

I continued for a short while longer and had a couple more casts until the wind started increasing and the rain started to fall.

Time to head home.

I'd had an enjoyable couple of hours on the bank caught some fish and got some exercise and some fresh air.

It was a good way to spend a morning.

TRIP DOWN MEMORY LANE

Location: Lancaster Canal, near Garstang

Date: 8th September 2023

Air Temp: 25°C

Background

I have very happy memories of fishing the Lancaster Canal. I first fished the canal when I was a teenager, travelling with my grandad to fish a junior match. I went on to fish it often, both for match fishing and for 'pleasure' fishing sessions.

The 'Lanky' is very different from my local Leeds and Liverpool Canal. It passes through miles of attractive countryside. It is narrower and shallower, and its banks seem to merge with the water. Reeds and occasional patches of waterlilies made it feel very special.

Forty years ago, the main species in the 'Lanky' were skimmers, 'Tommy' ruffe, eels, perch, and roach. The bigger bream were found in the wider parts of the canal, known as basins.

During this time, the Leeds and Liverpool Canal (in the area where I lived) had few skimmers and no ruffe. Roach, perch, and gudgeon were the dominant species.

For me, all these factors made the Lancaster Canal a fascinating and magical place to fish.

Fast forward to today, and I thought it was time for a trip down memory lane.

Conditions

A warm, cloudy day with sunny spells and patches of blue sky.

There were large rafts of floating weed on the canal and patches of weed underwater. The canal was quite clear but became a little more coloured as boat traffic increased.

Gear

Waggler rod, antenna float, 3lb mainline, 2lb hooklink, size 18 hook.

Bait

Red maggots, worms, sweetcorn and dark, natural groundbait.

Tactics

Loose feeding red maggots two rod lengths out and feeding groundbait and chopped worms across the canal.

The Fishing

I plumbed the peg and found it to be very shallow and weedy close in, so I decided to fish a little further out towards the middle of the canal.

Having seen a few fish 'blowing' (bubbling) on my nearside swim, I decided to feed very cautiously with red maggots.

I put a single red maggot on the hook and had my first cast.

Almost immediately, I had a bite. It was a small roach, and then another bite from a tiny perch.

The swim then went quiet.

This was to be the pattern for the day, catching one or two fish, and then the peg went quiet for long periods.

I continued to trickle in maggots, and fifteen minutes later, I had another bite, this time a bigger fish, a hybrid. This was followed by another hybrid of around 6 oz.

It was nice to catch hybrids. They always fight hard. I had heard that they were now present in the Lancaster Canal in large numbers. I'd not caught one on all my previous trips to the canal, all those years ago.

I always find it interesting how, over time, different species come and go. Some species can dominate for a while and then completely disappear.

Another cast, another fish, and then, as before, the swim went quiet.

A couple of boats sailed through the swim, and this added a slight tinge of colour to the canal. It also churned up some of the underwater weed.

When the water calmed, I fed a few more maggots.

After an hour's fishing, I had around eight fish: hybrids, roach, and perch.

I decided to introduce a small ball of groundbait laced with chopped worms across the canal.

I left this for half an hour to see if any fish would show up and settle on the feed.

I put a small worm on the hook and had several casts over the ground-baited swim, but without any success.

I continued to feed red maggots, fish red maggots on the hook, and fish my nearside swim. I tried single, double, and even triple red maggots on the hook and had bites on each.

Dragonflies buzzed my float tip, and swallows (or swifts?) did aerial displays in front of me, skimming the surface of the canal. The sun came out, and it was a wonderful day to be on the bank.

Although bites were sporadic, I loved every minute of being back on the 'Lanky'.

SUNDAY MORNING CHILL OUT

Location: Lancaster Canal, near Garstang

Date: 19th September 2023

Air Temp: 18°C

Background

Earlier in the month, I'd fished the Lancaster Canal and loved it.

I decided to return to have a relaxing Sunday morning session.

There are miles of canal, and many of them are great places to find solitude, away from the rat race. Few anglers fish the canal these days, and although there can be frequent boats passing through (especially during the summer), and the occasional walker, it's a place for peaceful fishing.

I went back to the stretch where I'd fished previously, but this time I walked further along the bank and found a nice, wide area (basin), which can hold shoals of bream.

Conditions

A very blustery, overcast day, feeling cold in the wind.

The canal was crystal clear at the start of the session, and it became more coloured as boats travelled through the swim.

Gear

Waggler rod, waggler, 3lb main line, varied hook sizes: size 18 to 2lb 8oz line; size 20 to 2lb line and size 22 to 1lb 8oz line.

Bait

Hookbaits: red maggots, worms and corn.

Feed: dark, natural groundbait, corn and hempseed.

Tactics

As I was fishing in a wide section of canal, which can often hold shoals of big skimmers and bream, my plan of attack was to fish two lines.

One: two-thirds of the way across the canal, where I would initially introduce a few balls of groundbait laced with corn. Two: a line, one and a half rod lengths out, where I would loose feed maggots and hempseed.

After feeding the ground-baited swim, I would leave this alone for an hour and start fishing on my nearside swim.

The Fishing

I fed a few maggots over my nearside swim, put a red maggot on the hook, and cast out my waggler float. It wasn't long before the float disappeared, and a nice roach of around 5 ounces was in the net.

I cast out and waited, but the swim had gone quiet. I trickled in a few more maggots and waited some more.

The facing wind had now strengthened and was making casting difficult, so I switched to a heavier float of the same antenna pattern I'd been using.

I loose fed a few grains of hemp.

After ten minutes, I had another bite. This time, a hybrid had taken my double-red maggot hookbait.

As appears to be the pattern on this stretch of canal, fish seem to come in ones and twos, and then the swim goes quiet for some time.

I swapped hook baits and hook sizes to try to improve my catch rate, but it didn't seem to make any difference.

My theory is that in the clear water, the fish 'spook' each time you catch a fish and take time to return.

After another period of inactivity, I caught a little perch on maggot and then had another lull.

I put a worm on the hook, thinking I might catch another perch, but I caught a roach instead.

After an hour, I decided to try my ground-baited swim. I cast out with a worm on the hook.

The colour of the sky reflected on the water's surface and the ripple made seeing the float tip difficult. A black-tipped float would have been ideal, but I didn't have one available, and I'd forgotten to bring my black permanent marker, which I use to blacken float tips.

Oh well, I'll just continue squinting at my float.

I added a few inches of depth to my rig, to counteract the wind and tow of the canal, in order to keep my bait pinned to the bottom. I also swapped to maggots on the hook.

I missed a couple of bites but then caught a roach and a perch in quick succession.

Then, a large barge decided to do a full 360° turn right in front of me, which churned up the canal, leaving enormous, dark clouds of silt hanging in the water.

How will this affect the fishing?

Once the churning and swirling of the canal had settled, I noticed that the canal was much less clear than it had been earlier.

I cast back over my ground-baited swim and almost immediately had a bite. This time it was from a palm-sized skimmer. Next cast: a roach.

I think that the murky water gave the fish more confidence.

The float sailed under again, and this time I had hooked heavy fish. A few seconds later, it came off. Undoubtedly a big skimmer or a bream. Arggh!

A little later, I had another bite, but it was a nice perch and not the hoped-for bream.

I fished on for a little while longer, but no more bream appeared.

Nevertheless, I'd had another lovely day's fishing on the Lancaster Canal and had learned a great deal. My keepnet contained roach, perch, a skimmer, and a few hybrids.

BREAD PUNCH FUN

Location: Leeds and Liverpool Canal, near Blackburn

Date: 18th November 2023

Air Temp: 11°C

Background

Bread is an inexpensive, easily accessible, and highly effective bait.

Breadpunch fishing involves using liquidised bread as feed (groundbait) and a pellet of bread on the hook (created by a breadpunch tool).

It is an excellent winter bait for roach and skimmers, and it can attract fish and get bites when other baits fail.

Bites often come immediately. Perfect when you want a few bites on the canal in wintertime.

Conditions

The weather wasn't yet wintry, but temperatures had been falling. With reduced boat traffic at this time of year, the water was very clear. It was a grey and dreary day with a cold breeze.

Gear

I'd loaded my two-wheel trolly with my Shakespeare seat box and my keepnet bag loaded with tackle. I used my waggler rod and small waggler float, 2.5lb mainline, and a size 22 hook to 1lb 8oz line.

Drennan punch set.

Bait

Feed: Liquidised bread - finely sieved.

Hookbaits: 2.5mm-4mm punched bread pellets.

Tactics

I fed a small ball of liquidised bread about the size of a conker in front of me, about a rod-and-a-half length out.

The liquidised bread suspended on the water's surface for a second and then fell through the water, leaving a streaming, white trail of attraction.

I used the rod like a whip, casting the float out with an underarm swing (and swinging in any fish I caught without winding my reel).

I use this technique when I want to catch fish quickly and efficiently but don't have my whips with me. It is also useful when fishing for small fish, but where there is a chance of bigger fish, which might be difficult to land using a whip.

The reel enables you to let a big fish run, rather than having to battle with them on a fixed line.

The Fishing

I started with a 3 mm punch. Just as the float settled, it went under. An instant response, which is often the case when breadpunch fishing.

I popped the small roach in my keepnet and again swung out my rig.

Another bite from a similar-sized roach.

So far, so good.

I continued to catch roach at a steady rhythm. When the swim went quiet, I fed another small ball of liquidised bread and the fish returned.

I tried different punch sizes, but the 2.5mm and 3mm were the most effective.

Sometimes, when punch fishing, you will have a fast start, but then the bites slow down, and you can eventually stop catching.

Today, the bites continued throughout the session, and I tallied up my catch using my 'clicker' (catch counter).

By the end of the session, I had 100 fish in the net. Good sport on a dreary November day.

USEFUL INFORMATION ABOUT FISHING ON CANALS

History of Canals in the UK

Canals are a network of artificial waterways throughout the UK. There are around two thousand miles of canals in the U.K.

Some canals date back to medieval and even Roman times, but many were constructed during the Industrial Revolution as a means of transporting goods using horse-drawn barges. Today, you can still see marks on the sides of bridges where ropes, which connected horses to the barges, have worn the bridge stones as they passed by.

The longest canals in the U.K. are the Grand Union Canal, which is 137 miles long, followed by the Leeds and Liverpool Canal, with a length of 127 miles.

The changing face of goods transport—the development of railways and the improved roads and motorway network—led to a decline in the amount of goods transported on canals. Numerous canals fell into decay.

Years later, there was an upsurge in canal use from recreational boaters, and canals were restored and redeveloped to meet this new demand.

Why Go Canal Fishing?

They are Widespread

There are over two thousand miles of canals spread throughout all parts of the UK. They pass through many built-up areas and through beautiful countryside. Chances are that you have a stretch of canal on your doorstep.

Inexpensive

Licences for canal fishing are often very inexpensive. Bait and equipment needed for canal fishing also won't break the bank and can be done on a tight budget.

Under-Fished

With the boom in popularity of commercial fisheries, canals are very lightly fished.

Home to Big Fish

This neglect has had a positive impact on the fish populations. Whereas, in the past, canals were typically regarded as small fish waters, today, good-quality fish of most species are present.

Great Scenery and Wildlife

Even in the most urban areas, canals can be scenic and home to lots of wildlife. Canals pass through miles of countryside, where you will find good fishing and also peace and tranquilly.

Characteristics of Canals

Depth

Many canals are shallow, being no deeper than 4-5 feet in the deepest parts, although some canals are much deeper. The deepest parts of the canal are known as the 'boat channel' or 'track.' This is often found down the middle of the canal but can be closer to the bank, on bends, or where other features divert the boats. The shallower parts of the canal tend to be close to the bank, where there is sometimes a shelf or a gradual slope towards the deepest parts of the canal.

Bottom

The bottom of the canals is often very silty, having built up over decades. There can be blanket weed covering the canal bed, and beds of weed might also be present. You need to take this into account before picking your fishing spot. Plumbing the depth will enable you to find the depth and help you find clear fishing spots.

Water Clarity

The clarity of the canal water usually depends on the amount of boat traffic on the stretch of canal. Boats churn up the silt, and this clouds the water. Regular boat traffic results in constantly murky water. When there is little or no boat traffic, the water tends to be much clearer.

Water flows into canals from various sources, including streams, which, after heavy rainfall, can colour the water.

Algae and other microorganisms also have an impact on water clarity. In warmer months, these add colour to canal water, and as they reduce in number over the cooler months, canal water becomes clearer.

Fishing canals with gin-clear water is often hard, as this makes the fish more wary and more difficult to catch.

The 'Tow'

Although canals seem to be mostly static, they flow; this is known as the 'tow.' The canal will tow most strongly when a boat approaches or nearby lock gates are opened. The wash from passing boats can sweep keepnets about, so a good tip when using keepnets while canal fishing is to use a cord to peg down the bottom end of your keepnet.

How to Find the Best Canal Fishing Spots

Walk the Canal Bank

When looking for suitable stretches of canals to fish, the easiest way is simply to go for a walk along your local canal's towpath and look for fish-holding features and active signs of fish.

You can spot jumping fish early in the morning and during the evening.

Wear Polarising Glasses to Locate Fish

Wearing a pair of polarising glasses cuts down on surface glare and enables you to see fish under the surface. It's surprising the difference this makes when trying to find fish.

Look for Features

It is worth taking the time to choose your spot. Look for fish-holding features such as lily pads, weeds, reeds, overhanging trees, etc. Wide parts of canals are known as basins and are good places to find shoals of bream.

Use Google Maps to find Fishing Spots

Google Maps is a good way to 'explore' potential canal fishing locations without leaving home. You can use your phone or computer to get a birds-eye view of stretches of canals and look for 'fishy-looking' stretches. You can use Google Maps to plan your travels and look for suitable access points to the canal.

Canal Fishing: Access Points and Parking

Access to canals is typically found near the bridges that span canals. There are access points at most bridges, although not always. Use Google Maps or visit the canal stretch prior to fishing. You can check access, including whether there are steps or narrow gate posts, which might make entering with a fishing trolly tricky.

Parking might also be limited for canal sections in the countryside. You might find that there is only space for a couple of vehicles next to the access points. A useful tip is to get to the canal early. So that you can park your car before these spaces are taken.

What Licences do I need to go Fishing on Canals?

1) Fishing Rod Licence

You'll need a Rod Licence before you fish in any inland waters. This licence, however, does not give you permission to fish anywhere. You still need to get permission to fish from the owner of the fishing rights or the angling club or organisation that controls the fishing on that water. There is no free fishing on canals.

Who needs to Buy a U.K. Rod Licence?

Anyone aged 13 or over. Parents or guardians of anyone under 13 if they're fishing too.

How much does a rod licence cost?

(As of April 1, 2023)

Standard (2 rods): £33

Standard (3 rods): £49.50

Junior (aged 13 to 16) is free, but you still must get a licence.

Over 65 or disabled: £22.

2) Permit to Fish the Particular Stretch of Canal

Local clubs rent out portions of the canal, and you may be able to purchase day tickets or an annual membership. To find out which licence you need, talk to local tackle shop owners and get their advice, or visit the stretch and check for notices that give fishing rules and information. You can also research canal fishing stretches online.

Waterways Wanderer Permit

For non-rented stretches, you will need to buy a Waterway Wanderers permit from the Canal and River Trust before you start to fish.

Costs for permits bought from April 1, 2023, onwards were:

Adult: £25. Concessions (includes concessionary rod licence holders, over 65s, or Angling Trust members*): £15. Juniors (aged 16 or under on the purchase date): £5

The Canal and River Trust website gives details of this scheme, including which canal stretches are covered, and you can buy permits online from them.

https://canalrivertrust.org.uk/things-to-do/fishing/where-to-fish/waterway-wanderers-scheme

Canal Fishing: What Fishing Equipment do I Need to go Canal Fishing?

The type of fishing equipment needed depends on which species you are targeting, and the techniques being used.

Basically, there are two main ways of fishing canals: the roving approach (lure fishing is a good example of this), where you are constantly moving, casting, and exploring a section of water. Alternatively, you can adopt a static approach and sit on a chair or seat box and fish in one spot.

Roving and Lure Fishing on Canals
Go Light

The secret to the lure-fishing roving approach is to travel light. A rod and reel, a landing net, a tackle bag, and an unhooking mat are all that you really need.

Roving allows you to cover lots of ground and explore stretches of canal when visiting it for the first time. You can also make a mental note of areas that you can come back to and fish with a static approach at a later date.

Techniques can include ultralight lure fishing, using tiny soft plastic lures, drop-shotting rigs, or tiny spinners. Rods should be short and light, coupled with small spinning or baitcasting reels. These outfits are good for targeting perch and can also be used to catch other silver-fish, such as roach and bream (which sometimes come as a surprise).

Bigger Predators

Stepping up from this are heavier outfits, which are capable of casting larger lures, like crankbaits, swimbaits, and large spinnerbaits. These are used to target bigger predators, like large perch and pike, and where they are present, zander.

Remember to use wire traces so that pike don't bite through your line, and take unhooking tools, including a good pair of forceps, for unhooking toothy predators.

Static Fishing on Canals

This is where you find a suitable place to fish and get comfortable on your chair or seat box. It can be a more relaxed way of fishing on canals and an enjoyable way to chill out.

Personally, unless you are a match angler and need to cover all canal fishing options, it is good to limit the amount of tackle that you take when canal fishing, even when fishing with a static approach.

My reasons for this are that you will make less bank-side noise, which is a vitally important aspect of fishing on these shallow waterways. Less gear means less effort and encourages you to walk further to find more out-of-the-way spots, which can hold more fish.

Less gear also means less clutter on the towpath, which is important when considering other canal users like walkers, dog walkers, joggers, and cyclists. Less gear also means that you are more likely to move if you are not catching anything. If, after a couple of hours, you aren't catching fish, moving to a new spot can help you find them. I like to use a small trolly to transport my fishing gear.

Canal Fishing: Fishing Rods and Tackle for Float Fishing on Canals

Fishing Rods, Reels and Lines

Most canals are narrow, so long casts are not needed. Rods in the ten- to twelve-foot range are ideal. Small reels and light lines (2–4 lb) are all you need when float fishing. A small waggler float is my go-to float for most conditions, stepping up to larger wagglers in windy conditions or when the canal is deep.

Hooks and Hook Sizes

The size of the fish targeted and the size of the hookbaits dictate the hook size. As a guide, when targeting roach and skimmer bream, use size 22 fine wire hooks for pinkies, size 20 fine wire hooks for single maggots, and size 18–16 fine wire hooks for double maggots and bread-punch.

Big Fish

Use heavier-gauge hooks when fishing for bigger fish, such as bream and tench, or fish with a bony mouth, like perch. Sizes 14–12 are useful for a single piece of corn. I'll use hooks up to size 10 when fishing worms, breadflake and double corn. Be aware that different brands hook sizes vary; they are not set sizes.

If you plan to target carp, a heavier line and stepped-up gear are needed.

Pole Fishing on Canals

Poles have many advantages when canal fishing. You can present your bait more accurately with less disturbance, and it allows you to fish in spots that would be impossible or difficult to cast using a rod and waggler setup.

By using a feed pot, you can feed much more accurately and with less disturbance. The use of light elastics means that lighter rigs and lines can be used.

Beware

An important consideration when pole fishing on canals is protecting your pole from passing cyclists, runners, and dogs. Many poles have been damaged by cyclists, runners, and dogs running into poles that have been 'dropped back' behind the angler when catching a fish, changing baits, or adjusting their rigs. It's important to check for approaching passersby when pushing your pole behind you.

Powerlines

Don't fish under powerlines at any time (even with a rod and reel).

Using Whips for Canal Fishing

Whips are lightweight poles, usually of a fixed length, with a length of line attached to the tip that is almost the same length as the whip. This enables you to swing out your rig and speedily swing in small fish.

Whips are ideal for catching smaller fish, such as roach, gudgeon, perch, and skimmers. Typically, whips used for canal fishing are in 2- to 4-metre lengths. Whip fishing is a simple method that can be used to amass large nets of small fish.

Floats tend to be heavier than standard pole floats because the weight of the float and its shot are used to swing or flick out your rig. Pencil-style floats are often used for whip fishing. Using a small waggler float can also be effective.

Ledgering on Canals

Ledgering can be an effective method for fishing canals. Short, lightweight feeder rods, or 'bomb' rods, are best. Use fibreglass quiver tips of an ounce or less to detect shy bites.

With canals having a silty bottom and being narrow, heavy leads or feeders are not needed. Small leads, tiny cage feeders, and small method feeders are best.

What are the Best Baits for Canal Fishing?

Hookbait and Loose Feeding

'Natural' baits, rather than pellets or boilies work best. Pellets and boilies can work, but they need to be used regularly by anglers for the canal fish to become accustomed to them.

You do not need enormous amounts of bait when canal fishing. For most fishing sessions, half a pint of pinkies, maggots, or casters is more than enough. Other useful baits are a small tin of sweetcorn, a tub of worms, or a few slices of bread (for breadpunch fishing). Hemp is a good loose feed and can be used on the hook or used with tares for hookbait, which are easier to hook.

Regularly loose-feeding small amounts of bait is an effective way to feed when canal fishing.

Groundbaits

Sometimes, the addition of groundbait in small quantities can attract and hold fish in your peg.

Instead of fishmeal-based groundbaits, go for natural groundbaits. Sensas, Sonubaits, and Bait-Tech sell non-fishmeal groundbaits that work well on canals.

An alternative and inexpensive choice that is highly effective on canals is liquidised bread combined with punched bread on the hook. Liquidise half a loaf of white bread (with or without crusts) in a blender or food processor and take a few slices of bread to use as hook bait.

Prebaiting Swims

An effective method of attracting and holding fish in particular areas is by prebaiting. This is where you feed bait into the swim for several days, or even weeks, before you go fishing.

This gets fish accustomed to feeding areas and particular baits. You might need to do this covertly so that other anglers don't pinch your spot!

Considering other Canal Users

As previously mentioned, non-anglers use the towpaths for a variety of activities. It is important to show them consideration when choosing a fishing spot and laying out your gear. It protects your fishing equipment from possible damage and potential accidents.

Dogs can be annoying when they stick their nose in your bait or try to steal your lunch! Keep lids on baits and secure any food that you take with you to prevent problems.

Boats are a regular feature on most canals. Boat traffic can be frequent during the summer months, but less so in the winter. If you want to avoid heavy boat traffic, fish in the early mornings or evenings.

Courteous boat owners will slow down as they approach you, while others will speed through your peg, creating a large wake and churning up the bottom. Although this is frustrating, the fish are used to it, and the added colour in the water can encourage shy fish to start feeding.

What are the Best Times to go Canal Fishing?

Fishing Season on Canals

You can fish all year on the majority of canals in the U.K. They are classified as still waters and do not have a closed season. Still, a few do have a closed season, and to find this, you need to check fishing club rules, the local tackle shop, or local bylaws online.

Best Time of Day to Go Fishing on Canals

Like most types of fishing, the most productive times to fish are early in the morning or in the evening. Canals are less busy, and fish feed more confidently at lower light levels.

Fish will feed throughout the day if the water is coloured, and the light levels are low. When the water is gin-clear and the sun is beating down, fishing can be difficult.

However, clear water conditions can be perfect for fishing for predators, which mainly hunt using their eyesight. Soft and hard plastic lures, or spinners, are easily seen and attacked in the clear water.

Canal Fishing: Summary

Canals offer good fishing that is easily accessible. There are hundreds of miles of canals in the U.K. You are likely to find stretches on your doorstep.

Canals are not heavily fished. You might be the only person fishing on a particular stretch of canal.

Canal fishing is ideal if you are on a budget. A small amount of inexpensive fishing tackle is all that you need. Bait is also cheap and easy to get hold of.

Light tackle and feeding 'little and often' are the keys to good sport.

When fishing on canals, you need to show consideration to other towpath users and boating enthusiasts. Most are friendly and like to say hello. Set up your gear off the towpath itself to prevent damage or accidents.

These days, many canals hold big fish, and there can be some pleasant surprises in store when you fish them. Canals should no longer be regarded as the home of small fish. Big bream, tench, and carp are often present.

Give canal fishing a go—you won't regret it!

You can find **more books by this author** by scanning the QR code below with your phone's camera (which will take you to the **Author's Amazon page**).

My website: www.000Fishing.com

My YouTube channel: https://www.youtube.com/@000fishing

YOUR NOTES

Printed in Great Britain
by Amazon

40800556R00066